BIRDS MAGIC MOMENTS

MARKUS VARESVUO

First published in 2011 by New Holland Publishers
London ● Cape Town ● Sydney ● Auckland
www.newhollandpublishers.com

Garfield House, 86-88 Edgware Road, London W2 2EA, United Kingdom
80 McKenzie Street, Cape Town, 8001, South Africa
Unit 1, 66 Gibbes Street, Chatswood, NSW 2067, Australia
218 Lake Road, Northcote, Auckland, New Zealand

10 9 8 7 6 5 4 3 2 1

A CIP catalogue record for this book is available from the British Library.

ISBN 978 1 78009 075 7

Publisher: Simon Papps
Design: Nicola Liddiard
Translation: Minna Lindroth
Production: Melanie Dowland

Reproduction by Pica Digital PTE Ltd, Singapore
Printed and bound in China By Toppan LeeFung Printing Ltd

WILD WONDERS
OF EUROPE

The following images are used courtesy of
Wild Wonders of Europe – © Markus
Varesvuo / Wild Wonders of Europe
(*www.wild-wonders.com*):

pages 24 (Red-footed Falcon), 27 (Roller),
40 and 55 (Starling), 41 (Chaffinch),
59, 61 and 110 (European Bee-eater),
108 (Turtle Dove) and 157 (Hoopoe).

GYR FALCON
Falco rusticolus

An intensely blue sky, light reflecting off the
snow and an inquisitive Gyr Falcon coming
to check up on the photographer make a
perfect combination.

BLUETHROAT
Luscinia svecica

The ground is still partly covered by snow
and the dwarf birches are in bud when
the males arrive on their breeding
territories. They advertise their presence
by singing loudly and eagerly from good
vantage points.

BIRDS MAGIC MOMENTS

MARKUS VARESVUO

NEW HOLLAND

CONTENTS

STELLER'S EIDER
Polysticta stelleri

In winter, sheltered fishing harbours can draw lots of seabirds to feed on fish guts. This makes the piers and wharves good places for photography. Dark water in the background serves to emphasize the strong coloration of this male.

WILLOW GROUSE
Lagopus lagopus

These grouse tend to feed in the mornings and evenings, spending the middle of the day burrowed fully or partly into the snow. This provides good insulation against the cold and wind and makes it harder for predators to spot them in the open habitats they frequent.

LAMMERGEIER
Gypaetus barbatus

The importance of background cannot be overestimated. This photo shows a Lammergeier in its habitat: caught gliding high in the air against a backdrop of its home cliffs in the snow-covered mountains of southern Europe.

I have watched birds since I was a child and the magic has not worn any thinner, quite the opposite in fact.

Photography soon became a part of the watching game, and it is both the means and the end in itself. Would I take pictures if I did not have an audience? Yes! Do I like to share my work? Yes again.

Firstly, photography is about capturing great moments, like mass migration or the majestic flight of a Lammergeier against an imposing Pyrenean peak. Or a Common Redstart posing in front of the camera like the most graceful ballerina. Or the intense, heated action in a Black Grouse lek.

It is always about finding the next great moment. And then it is about the challenge of successfully capturing the moments. Making dreams come true.

The unpredictability is stimulating. You can't grow tired of something that keeps changing all the time. At least for me, the balance between being disappointed and feeling like I am on top of the world has been perfect – just the right amount of disappointments to keep the successes sweet and a delightful number of successes to keep me going from one hurdle to the next.

You can make the best of plans and get zero pictures or, by sheer luck, stumble into a fantastic opportunity and get super shots. Success is never guaranteed, there is always a challenge. It is a hunt.

Birds are part of our world and we need them, more than they need us. I think we also need their magic. How much more boring would the world be without them?

Birds are a good excuse to get out and enjoy the very rich natural life out there, be it deep in the woods, somewhere in the middle of nowhere, on a beautiful lake or in the middle of our cities, in our parks and on roofs and pavements.

MARKUS VARESVUO

CAPERCAILLIE
Tetrao urogallus

To witness a Capercaillie lek at close range is a fantastic experience where sound plays a major role. Especially in the early days of the lek, the males compete and spar with each other. As the spring progresses, females arrive to choose a mate; usually the alpha-male.

BLACK GROUSE
Tetrao tetrix

Completely calm conditions are needed to capture the breath of a lekking Black Grouse wheezing on a cold winter's morning. To get good photographs, you also need a dark background and backlight so that the swirling breath is caught on the camera sensor.

NORTHERN WHEATEAR
Oenanthe oenanthe

Some male passerines perform a song flight in order to catch a female's attention. This is done through a combination of sound plus special flight patterns or showing eye-catching feathers such as the white in a wheatear's tail.

GOLDENEYE
Bucephala clangula

When displaying, the male gives a grating call, tosses its head and splashes water with its webbed feet. The females seem to find this attractive!

RED-NECKED GREBE
Podiceps grisegena

To a human ear, the grebes' display duet sounds awful, but the wailing, squealing and bellowing while engaged in a co-ordinated dance are an essential part of forging a pair-bond between the male and female.

COMMON GULL
Larus canus

As the pair gives its laughing *kay-a kay-a kay-a kay-a ke ke* duet, backlight, the symmetry in the birds' positions and the ice make this picture interesting.

HERRING GULL
Larus argentatus

Landing with due pomp in a colony, this male is signalling to his partner that she has chosen well and to his rivals that they should keep well away from his mate.

THRUSH NIGHTINGALE
Luscinia luscinia

Quintessential signs of summer in
north-east Europe – a singing Thrush
Nightingale and a blossoming apple tree.

COMMON NIGHTINGALE
Luscinia megarhynchos

For attracting attention nightingales use
full-throated vocals over fancy feathers.
During the breeding season, this usually
rather secretive bird can sometimes be
seen serenading on an open branch.

VELVET SCOTER
Melanitta fusca

Spring flocks gather in a sheltered bay, from where small groups regularly break off to make short, vocal flypasts over the nesting islands. The birds have already paired up, but the males still have the occasional skirmish.

SLAVONIAN GREBE
Podiceps auritus

These birds were onto their second brood one August when a sudden storm caused the water level to rise rapidly and threaten their nest, leading to some emergency rebuilding.

RUFF
Philomachus pugnax

On migration in early May the birds stop
to rest on the best wader shores in
southern Finland. Already well into their
display, the males parade regally in front of
the females showing their fantastic feather
collars. This female is lowering herself to a
mating position.

SLAVONIAN GREBE
Podiceps auritus

Having performed their display dancing, and selected their partners, the grebes start building their floating nests. When the structure is ready it is time to mate, and this often takes place on the nest.

RED-FOOTED FALCON
Falco vespertinus

As with many raptor species, the female calls out loudly to the male, demanding copulation. To strengthen her demand, she gets down into a mating position. During the most intense laying period, the pair mates several times a day.

GREY PHALAROPE
Phalaropus fulicarius

In the shallow waters of a delta, the female, which is more colourful than the male, lowers herself into position to signal to the male that it is time to mate.

ROLLER
Coracias garrulus

As part of their display routine the male brings food gifts to the female. If the gift pleases her, and the moment is right, she will indicate her willingness to mate.

RED-THROATED DIVER
Gavia stellata

Since they like to nest in small marshy ponds that usually have no fish, the parents bring food for their chicks from nearby lakes. Landing into a headwind, the parent returns with a spectacular splash into the water. The small chicks can swallow amazingly big fish as whole.

SNOWY OWL
Bubo scandiaca

On the Arctic tundra, if a crash in the lemming population coincides with the owls' breeding season it can cause most of the young to perish. Some pairs hunt a more varied prey, bringing birds to the chicks if there are no more lemmings.

SWALLOW
Hirundo rustica

Swallows continue to feed their young for a few days after they have learnt to fly. Here a fledgling is resting on a branch between flight and hunting practices, and is being fed by its parent.

RED-THROATED PIPIT
Anthus cervinus

The pipits time their nesting on the Arctic tundra so that the insect population is at its peak just when the young are hatching. This enables them to raise relatively large broods of five or six chicks.

SLAVONIAN GREBE
Podiceps auritus

The parents often carry their young on
their backs, where they are kept warmer
and safer from predators than if they were
swimming on their own. This chick is
already almost too big to travel in such a
piggyback style.

GOLDEN PLOVER
Pluvialis apricaria

As with many other waders, this species
performs a 'broken wing' display to lure
enemies away from its young. When the
predator turns its attention to the 'lame'
parent, the latter starts to lead it further
away from the young, leaving them hiding
safely in the undergrowth.

COMMON CRANE
Grus grus

Sometimes persistent hide-squatting
pays off. Luckily the wind was in the right
direction to stop the fox from scenting
the photographer. The fox had its eye on
the crane's nest and eggs, but the bird was
not intimidated and crossed the pond to
chase it away.

GREEN WOODPECKER
Picus viridis

Birds need water to drink and to wash.
Clean, healthy feathers are vital to an
individual's well-being, especially for
regulating body temperature and for flying.

ROBIN
Erithacus rubecula

Using slow shutter speed and positioning
the bird in backlight helped create an effect
where the water drops raised by the
bathing young Robin formed golden arches
in the picture.

STARLING
Sturnus vulgaris

The Starlings arrive en masse at the drinking ponds at sunset. A slow shutter speed left some movement in the birds as they jostled each other to get to the best spots for bathing.

CHAFFINCH
Fringilla coelebs

The last, soft light at dusk is good for photographing a bathing Chaffinch; the white wing-patch doesn't get overexposed and the light does justice to the bird's beautiful coloration.

GOSHAWK
Accipiter gentilis

The hawk is extremely cautious when approaching water, staying in a nearby tree for a long time, assessing the situation before deciding it is safe to come and drink. It reaches down to fill its bill with water and as it lifts its head to drink, some of the water always trickles back into the pool.

GOOSANDER
Mergus merganser

A female has caught a ruffe, which is coveted by another bird. The ensuing furious chase along the surface of the water is captured using a relatively slow shutter speed, emphasizing the movement.

BLACK GROUSE
Tetrao tetrix

Photographing the males in their display
fights is thrilling. The action is so fast that
apart from trying to make sure that the
location is perfect, timing is good and
weather favourable, a photographer cannot
do much more than keep shooting in serial
mode and hope for good results.

GREY HERON
Ardea cinerea

The herons arrive in their breeding areas in southern Finland in March, when most water is still frozen. Food is scarce and any surplus fish left over by fishermen can cause fierce squabbles.

SLAVONIAN GREBE
Podiceps auritus

A good nesting site is worthy of a fight amongst the males. When the rivals are well matched, the skirmishes can last several days before a winner emerges.

RED KITE
Milvus milvus

One kite is trying to snatch another's catch. After a short fight in the air, the raider gives up and the original hunter gets to keep the prey.

WHITE-TAILED EAGLE AND COMMON GULL
Haliaeetus albicilla **and** *Larus canus*

The gull uses its agility and swiftness against the eagle's superior strength and size when trying to defend its nest.

GOLDEN EAGLE
Aquila chrysaetos

During long cold spells in mid-winter, carcasses offered to predators by photographers can attract up to half a dozen eagles. The rule of the fittest determines the feeding order – the weaker ones don't eat until the strongest have sated their hunger.

HOODED CROW
Corvus cornix

Snow and ice often make finding food a problem for birds, so these crows are fighting over who gets the juicy fish guts.

STARLING
Sturnus vulgaris

Birds fight over many things, including mates, nesting territories and food, but this squabble is over bathing rights.

HERRING GULL
Larus argentatus

Gulls must be near the top of the list of
easy subjects. They are relatively fearless
and easily lured to desired locations with
food. In this image, backlight and a dark
background help bring out the white gulls
and the splashing water.

GREAT CRESTED GREBE
Podiceps cristatus

The calm water, refection of the arching
neck and the eye of the diving grebe visible
through the water all add to this picture.

EUROPEAN BEE-EATER
Merops apiaster

At the beginning of their breeding season,
bee-eater males bring mating gifts to their
partners. This male offered a handsome
dragonfly to the female as she landed on
the branch to take a rest from nest-digging
activities.

EUROPEAN BEE-EATER
Merops apiaster

It requires a lot of persistence and luck to take a picture of a bee-eater that is just about to catch an insect (above). The bird will then return to its favourite perch with its prey (right), which it kills by beating it against the branch and then tossing it into the air to align it for easy swallowing. To capture this moment took an intense shooting session lasting a couple of days.

WHITE-TAILED EAGLE
Haliaeetus albicilla

In some areas, the eagles have learnt to take surplus fish tossed back into the sea by fishermen or fish offered by photo tour guides. Such settings offer great opportunities for photographers.

■□

OSPREY
Pandion haliaetus

A male Osprey returns to the nest with a roach for the young. As the offspring grow, they need more food every passing day.

□■

OSPREY
Pandion haliaetus

A different approach to an Osprey picture. A male is landing on the nest, clutching the prey it had caught for the young. The head of the fish is visible from behind the bird's tail.

Ospreys can catch fish that are as deep as one metre underwater. In such instances just their wing-tips remain above the surface. The dive lasts only the briefest of moments before the bird re-emerges and takes off into a headwind, clutching its prey.

BAR-TAILED GODWIT
Limosa lapponica

Young waders are often quite fearless and a photographer can get relatively close to foraging birds without a hide. The best shots of this godwit were taken when it waded in the surf looking for food in the shallow water.

KNOT
Calidris canutus

Sometimes the waves broke over the seaweed and I tried to capture the feeding birds as they were ducking and dodging the sudden splashes. The flying seaweed and water created an interesting background of turmoil.

RED-NECKED PHALAROPE
Phalaropus lobatus

These birds usually catch their insect prey from the water's surface, but at times they can also chase and catch them in the air.

■□

GREAT SKUA AND ARCTIC TERN
Stercorarius skua **and** *Sterna paradisaea*

Although skuas are great hunters, terns are usually too fast and agile for them. But this skua was smart. It waited for the tern to dive after fish and positioned itself right above, catching it as it came out of the water.

□■

MARSH HARRIER
Circus aeruginosus

I experiment a lot with ice and snow as elements in my pictures. Here, even though there is only a mere glimpse of ice between the reed stalks, it reflects light back into the air, beautifully highlighting the hunting harrier's underside.

ARCTIC TERN
Sterna paradisaea

Taken at the outlet of a glacier lake, a hint of the greenish light reflecting off the ice hits the hovering tern, which is ready to plunge into the water and fish.

LITTLE GULL
Hydrocoloeus minutus

In early summer, these gulls fly very close to water's surface and dip down to catch recently hatched insects. The moment is very fast and surprisingly difficult to capture (*above*). In an alternative technique, the gulls will fly into a strong wind, stopping at times to tread the water with their webbed feet and catch insects in their bill (*right*).

GREAT GREY OWL
Strix nebulosa

In late winter, the owls often hunt in open fields if the woods run out of voles. The birds can be quite fearless and if a photographer waits patiently it is possible to get pictures of an authentic hunt (*above*). Some individuals learn to come to bait such as small pieces of meat (*left*).

GREAT GREY OWL
Strix nebulosa

This picture is lifted beyond just a basic flight shot due to the owl's intense gaze, majestically spread wings and shadow, together with the backlight, light reflecting off the snow and the contrast of the blue tint of the snow in the shadow and the pure white of the snow in the sunshine.

GREAT GREY OWL
Strix nebulosa

Thanks to its rounded wings and soft feathers, the owl can fly completely silently and surprise its prey. Silence is also essential as the owl relies upon hearing its prey scurrying under the snow. It can sink its long legs as deep as 50cm into the snow to catch a vole.

HAWK OWL
Surnia ulula

These owls range over large areas in autumn, settling only when they have found a site with sufficient numbers of voles (*right*). Hawk Owls cannot reach prey deep under the snow, so relying on excellent eye-sight they wait patiently in an open spot until a vole emerges and they can fly down after it (*opposite*).

GREAT GREY SHRIKE
Lanius excubitor

Shrikes perch on good vantage points,
looking for prey. Once they have spotted
something, they fly to it and hover until they
feel that the moment is right for the kill.

HOODED CROW
Corvus cornix

These crows are opportunists, eating almost anything. They have learnt to scour human refuse for food. This liquor bottle yielded little foodwise but it entertained the bird for quite some time.

DIPPER
Cinclus cinclus

Dippers forage in streams by either diving and walking on river beds or swimming on the surface and dipping their heads under. Sometimes they emerge without a catch (*left*), but frequently the hunting is successful (*above*).

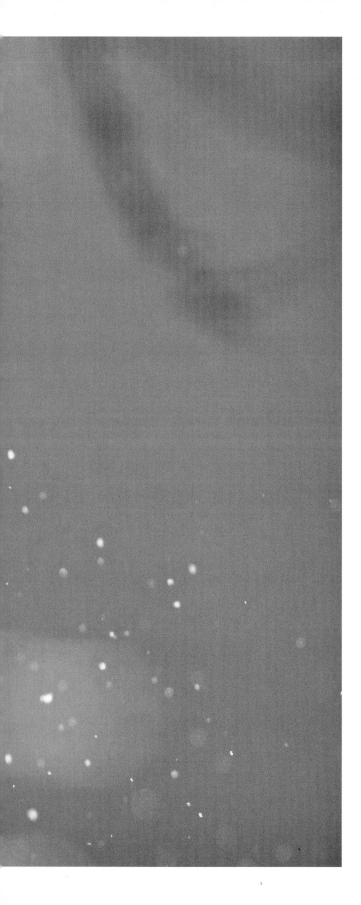

WAXWING
Bombycilla garrulus

Waxwings are very skilful at picking berries, sometimes balancing on a branch or bunch of berries, sometimes hovering to pick at them. Here the bird missed its target.

WAXWING
Bombycilla garrulus

The berry bunches are heavy, hanging on the tips of thin branches, which requires good acrobatic skills to get at them (*left*). The Waxwings swallow the berries whole (*above*) but digest only the flesh. The seeds pass through, so the birds help the rowans to distribute them.

GREENFINCH
Carduelis chloris

Rosehips are one of this species' favourite foods in the autumn, and the remnants of the meal can often be seen around their bills.

GOLDFINCH
Carduelis carduelis

In winter, bur and thistle seeds form a significant part of the Goldfinch's diet. This bird is captured against the background of a red house.

GOLDCREST
Regulus regulus

These tiny birds can often be spotted hovering at the tips of branches looking for spiders and insects.

YELLOW-BROWED WARBLER
Phylloscopus inornatus

This warbler is a rare visitor to Europe from the east. Like Goldcrests they can hover in order to glean invertebrate food.

COMMON CROSSBILL
Loxia curvirostra

When snow coats the trees in thick layers, crossbills have to work hard to get food. When the cone is finally dug out of the snow, they use their strong bill to snap it off and carry it to a suitable branch where they can eat the seeds.

SHOVELER
Anas clypeata

Two males are chasing a female, competing against each other to win her attention at the start of the breeding season.

LONG-TAILED DUCK
Clangula hyemalis

The male (left) dragged its very long tail along the water's surface, while the female (below) tumbled softly on the ice and was able to recover its footing.

KING EIDER
Somateria spectabilis

A photographer benefits from knowing that all large waterbirds take off into a headwind to get as much air under their wings as possible.

GRIFFON VULTURE
Gyps fulvus

A cloudy sky and light reflecting off the snow and hitting the bird's underside helped to create studio-like lighting conditions where the vulture is evenly lit from all angles.

SHAG
Phalacrocorax aristotelis

To reduce speed for landing the bird fully spreads its wings and opens its tail as widely as possible. Even the webbed feet are used as breaks.

GOSHAWK
Accipiter gentilis

The hawk's hunting strategy is based mostly on surprise and stealth; its chances of catching birds through open pursuit are not so good.

RAZORBILL
Alca torda

As the bird comes in to land on its nesting cliff, a long tele-lens used to take this picture blends the grey ocean in the distance into a pleasantly uniform background.

TURTLE DOVE
Streptopelia turtur

The dove attempts to land in a small
pool of water to bathe, but while hovering
it seems to realise that the water is too
deep and returns to the edge to
re-evaluate the situation.

BEARDED TIT
Panurus biarmicus

The bird's short wings are perfectly suited
for short spurts of flight inside the dense
reedbeds it inhabits.

EUROPEAN BEE-EATER
Merops apiaster

Even a champion hunter sometimes ends up empty-billed. A bee-eater returns to its partner after an unsuccessful hunting trip.

COMMON REDSTART
Phoenicurus phoenicurus

This male redstart is just about to push up from a branch to its nest with a juicy caterpillar to feed to the young.

PTARMIGAN
Lagopus muta

During winter, these grouse live in flocks or small groups. In mid-April these break up and the pairs spread out to their nesting territories. Here, just before the beginning of breeding season, one male lands next to another.

PUFFIN
Fratercula arctica

Returning to its nesting cliff, and landing
into a headwind, a Puffin almost stops in
mid-air before gracefully touching down on
the ground.

LAMMERGEIER
Gypaetus barbatus

A dream came true when photographing Lammergeiers in the majestic mountains of the Pyrenees, with snowy conditions and beautiful sunshine creating fantastic settings for the flying birds.

ARCTIC SKUA
Stercorarius parasiticus

In northern Norway the sun does not set at all in midsummer, and the midnight sun casts a special, golden light which illuminates the skua as it flies against a dark mountain in the background.

◼◻

SPARROWHAWK
Accipiter nisus

Many headlands along migration routes are good spots for photographing raptors. Finland's Hanko Point is a good example. Thousands of Sparrowhawks pass each autumn and some of them, like this adult male, fly right past the photographer.

◻◼

BLACK WOODPECKER
Dryocopus martius

A combination of backlight edging the bird and light reflecting off the snowy bank underneath lighting it evenly, plus a dark blue background in the form of a shady hillside and light snow falling from a tree above has made this Black Woodpecker picture a little different.

HOOPOE
Upupa epops

Sometimes good pictures are the result of careful preparation, or patience and perseverance, and other times they just happen, a bit like snapshots. I was in a park when I noticed a group of people about to pass this Hoopoe. I knew it would take off. It did and I was ready.

MAGPIE
Pica pica

For a bird that looks superficially black and white, a Magpie's coloration is surprisingly rich when seen in the right light and with wings spread out.

■□

SIBERIAN JAY
Perisoreus infaustus

These amiable, inquisitive and bold birds come readily to food, and in return they give many photo opportunities as they fly off to hide their loot in the forest.

□■

SNOW BUNTING
Plectrophenax nivalis

The ground is still mostly snow-covered when the birds first arrive at their breeding sites in spring. The few open patches draw the birds to feed in big flocks, offering many good chances for taking pictures.

LONG-TAILED DUCK
Clangula hyemalis

On some May days several hundred thousand Long-tailed Ducks migrate along the coast of the Gulf of Finland towards their breeding grounds. The migration escalates as the day progresses, often continuing through the night.

COMMON CRANE
Grus grus

The fading light colours the evening and the migrating cranes in shades of pink, purple and blue.

◻▪

COMMON SCOTER
Melanitta nigra

The scoters migrate in May, heading to their Arctic breeding sites. They fly through the night at times, and are caught here against the Moon.

WOODPIGEON
Columba palumbus

From a photographic point of view, the best wind for the autumn migration is a headwind as it forces the birds to fly low.

BRAMBLING
Fringilla montifringilla

Bramblings gather on open fields in autumn to feed up ahead of migration. Sometimes they flock in thousands, nervously taking off at every alarm caused by a Sparrowhawk or other threat.

STELLER'S EIDER
Polysticta stelleri

These smart ducks inhabit northern fishing harbours in the winter to take advantage of their shelter and the discarded fish guts.

COMMON GUILLEMOT
Uria aalge

Seabirds have just arrived on their breeding cliffs on Hornøya island in northern Norway. The nesting season has not yet begun, and they are unconcerned by a photographer, which makes it possible to use a wide-angle lens.

BARNACLE GOOSE
Branta leucopsis

The geese flock together in autumn to forage on open fields before flying to their roosting rocks out at sea late in the evening. This picture is taken with almost no light and no intention to freeze any movement. Instead it portrays the atmosphere of a huge flock taking off in moonlight.

RAVEN
Corvus corax

Ravens are extremely cautious and keen-sighted birds. In winter they gather in flocks at the best feeding sites. There is always one bird in a flock that spots something suspicious and raises an alarm that lets the flock escape a Golden Eagle (*above*) or Goshawk raid.

PTARMIGAN
Lagopus muta

Ptarmigans blend in perfectly with their background whatever the time of year. This chick (*above*) had wandered into the ruins of an old lodge, but even here its camouflage worked well against the lichen-covered timber. The white winter plumage of the adults makes it hard for predators to spot them (*right*).

PTARMIGAN
Lagopus muta

The adult's greyish summer plumage is perfect camouflage in their habitat of grey rock and Arctic vegetation.

SNOWY OWL
Bubo scandiaca

The female owl is white with brown markings in all seasons. They blend well into the snow in winter but can also be amazingly difficult to spot sitting on a nest on the ground in the green summer surroundings.

WATER RAIL
Rallus aquaticus

It is very rare to find Water Rails attempting to winter in Finland. If a big enough body of water remains open all year, then they can survive.

HERRING GULL
Larus argentatus

Weather changes are rapid on the Varanger Peninsula in northern Norway. A fierce snowstorm comes to an end as the sun shines onto the gulls through the dark clouds, creating a dramatic scene that suits a photographer.

■□

RINGED PLOVER
Charadrius hiaticula

Rising winds kept raising the water level and building the waves until this small group of plovers grew tired of trying to avoid them and decided to move to a more sheltered spot.

□■

ALPINE ACCENTOR
Prunella collaris

Accentors are hardened birds, moving
down from the mountains only when
absolutely everything is covered by snow.
They will remain as long as small patches
stay open.

KITTIWAKE
Rissa tridactyla

Snowstorms offer great shooting
opportunities. Here is a Kittiwake captured
in heavy snowfall, photographed against the
dark sea far in the background.

GRIFFON VULTURE
Gyps fulvus

Pure white snow and a snowstorm aren't the most common settings for these vultures but they manage well even in these circumstances as long as there is food.

■□

HAWK OWL
Surnia ulula

Thirty degrees below freezing does not bother a Hawk Owl too much as long as there are voles to hunt.

□■

LAMMERGEIER
Gypaetus barbatus

A young bird in the process of alighting;
the blackish head and mottled brown
underparts distinguish it from the adults.

VELVET SCOTER
Melanitta fusca

A close-up of a pair, with the brown female in the foreground and the black male behind.

COMMON CRANE
Grus grus

The call is loud and carries for miles in good weather. Photographers can still hear the sound ringing in their ears long into the night after a day spent near cranes.

COMMON GUILLEMOT
Uria aalge

Seabird colonies are great for photography as there are always birds coming and going. The photographer has an embarrassment of riches and very tight close-ups are possible.

GREAT GREY OWL
Strix nebulosa

The owl's face is shaped with one thing in mind – to collect as much sound information as possible. Although it has very keen eyesight, an excellent sense of hearing is more important when hunting voles under the snow in winter.

GOLDEN EAGLE
Aquila chrysaetos

Arctic Hares form a vital part of this
species' diet in the winter. Here an adult
eagle is plucking a hare to get to the meat.

HOOPOE
Upupa epops

The crown feathers are opened when the
bird is alarmed or excited. They are also
raised for a second or two after landing.
Here a parent brings food for the young.

Images listed by page number. All photographs are taken in Finland using a Canon EOS camera unless otherwise stated.

1 1Ds mk III, 500 mm + 1.4x extender, f6.3, 1/2000s, ISO 800 *April 2009, Norway*

3 1Ds mk II, 500 mm + 1.4x extender, f5.6, 1/320s, ISO 320 *June 2005*

4 1D mk II, 500 mm, f4.5 1/2000s, ISO 400 *April 2006, Norway*

5 1Ds mk II, 500 mm + 1.4x extender, f16, 1/1000s, ISO 400 *April 2007*

6 1D mk IV, 500 mm, f8, 1/2000s, ISO 800 *November 2010, Spain*

8 1D, 300 mm, f11, 1/100s, ISO 200 *April 2003*

9 1D, 300 mm, f2.8, 1/400s, ISO 200 *April 2003*

10 1D mk II, 500 mm, f5.6, 1/3200s, ISO 500 *May 2006*

11 1D mk II, 500 mm + 1.4x extender, f6.3, 1/1600s, ISO 320 *April 2006*

12 1Ds mk II, 500 mm, f9, 1/1000s, ISO 250 *May 2005*

13 1D mk II, 500 mm, f5.6, 1/400s, ISO 400 *April 2006*

14 1Ds mk III, 500 mm, f11, 1/2000s, ISO 500 *April 2008*

16 1D mk II, 500 mm + 1.4x extender, f5.6, 1/200 mm, ISO 400 *May 2005, Estonia*

17 1D mk II, 500 mm, f9, 1/100s, ISO 400 *May 2006, Hungary*

18 & 19 1D mk IV, 800 mm, f5.6, 1/1000s, ISO 1250 *May 2010*

20 & 21 1Ds mk III, 800 mm, f5.6 (20)/ f10 (21), 1/1000s, ISO 800 *August 2009*

22 1Ds mk III, 800 mm, f9, 1/500s, ISO 500 *May 2009*

23 1D mk IV, 800 mm, f7.1, 1/500s, ISO 800 *May 2010*

24 1D mk III, 300 mm, f5, 1/1600s, ISO 1600 *May 2008, Hungary*

25 1Ds mk II, 500 mm + 1.4x extender, f6.3, 1/400s, ISO 400 *June 2006, Iceland*

26 1D mk II, 300 mm, f3.2, 1/1250s, ISO 500 *May 2007, Hungary*

27 1D mk III, 300 mm, f4, 1/2000s, ISO 1600 *May 2008, Hungary*

28 1D mk III, 500 mm, f4, 1/800s, ISO 1600 *June 2009*

29 1D mk III, 500 mm, f4 , 1/1600s, ISO 2000 *June 2009*

30 1D mk III, 500 mm + 2.0x extender, f9, 1/1000s, ISO 2000 *July 2007*

32 1D mk II, 500 mm, f4, 1/2000s, ISO 640 *July 2005*

33 1D mk II, 500 mm, f4, 1/2000s, ISO 400 *June 2005, Norway*

34 1Ds mk III, 800 mm, f11, 1/100s, ISO 800 *August 2009*

35 1D mk II, 500 mm, f6.3, 1/640s, ISO 400 *June 2005, Norway*

36 & 37 1D mk II, 300 mm, f5.6, 1/200s, ISO 400 *May 2005*

38 1D mk III, 500 mm, f4, 1/4000s, ISO 1250 *December 2008, Spain*

39 1D mk II, 500 mm, f22, 1/10s, ISO 500 *July 2006, Hungary*

40 1D mk III, 300 mm, f5.6, 1/50s, ISO 1600 *May 2008, Hungary*

41 1D mk III, 500 mm, f6.3, 1/400s, ISO 1250 *May 2008, Hungary*

42 1D mk II, 500 mm + 1.4x extender, f5.6, 1/400s, ISO 1000 *May 2007, Hungary*

43 1Ds mk II, 300 mm, f3.5, 1/2000s, ISO 800 *May 2007, Hungary*

44 1D mk II, 500 mm + 1.4x extender, f13, 1/160s, ISO 400 *April 2006*

45 above 1D mk III, 500 mm, f4.5, 1/2000s, ISO 1600 *March 2008*

45 below 1D mk III, 500 mm, f4, 1/800s, ISO 1600 *April 2008*

46 1D mk II, 500 mm+ 1.4x extender, f5.6, 1/1000s, ISO 500 *March 2007*

48 1D mk III, 800 mm, f7.1, 1/3200s, ISO 2000 *May 2009*

49 1Ds mk III, 800 mm + 1.4x extender, f8, 1/2000s, ISO 800 *December 2009, Spain*

50 & 51 1D mk IV, 500 mm, f10 (50) and f6.3 (51), 1/2500s, ISO 1000 *July 2010, Norway*

52 1D mk II, 300 mm, f4, 1/1000s, ISO 800 *February 2007*

54 1Ds mk II , 500 mm + 1.4 extender, f7.1, 1/1000s, ISO 400 *March 2007*

55 1D mk III, 300 mm, f2.8, 1/1600s, ISO 1600 *May 2008, Hungary*

56 1D mk II 300 mm, f6.3, 1/1600 s, ISO 400 *August 2005, Norway*

58 1Ds mk II, 500 mm + 1.4x extender, f10, 1/1000s, ISO 400 *April 2007*

59 1Ds mk III, 500 mm + 1.4x extender, f11, 01/500s, ISO 500 *May 2008, Hungary*

60 1D mk III, 800 mm, f9, 1/2000s, ISO 1250 *May 2009, Israel*

61 1D mk III, 500 mm, f6.3, 1/2000s, ISO 1600 *May 2008, Hungary*

62 1D mk IV, 500 mm, f4.5, 1/2000s, ISO 1600 *July 2010, Norway*

63 1Ds mk III, 500 mm, f7.1, 1/1000s, ISO 800 *June 2008*

64 1D mk III, 500 mm, f7.1, 1/1600s, ISO 1600 *June 2008*

66 1D mk III, 300 mm, f8, 1/3200s, ISO 1250 *April 2009*

68 1D mk II, 500 mm, f14, 1/1250s, ISO 500 *September 2006*

69 1D mk IV, 500 mm, f11, 1/800s, ISO 800 *August 2010*

70 1D mk II, 500 mm, f8, 1/2000s, ISO 800 *June 2006, Iceland*

71 1D mk II, 500 mm, f6.3, 1/2000s, ISO 500 *June 2006, Iceland*

72 1D mk II 500 mm, f4.0, 1/1600 s, ISO 400 *April 2006*

73 1D mk II, 500 mm, f5.6, 1/1600s, ISO 500 *June 2006, Iceland*

74 1D mk II, 500 mm, f4.5, 1/2500s, ISO 160 *June 2004, Latvia*

75 1D mk II, 500 mm, f4.5, 1/2500s, ISO 320 *May 2005*

76 1D mk III, 14 mm, f6.3, 1/2000s, ISO 1600 *March 2009*

77 1D mk IV, 200 mm, f5.6, 1/2000s, ISO 1250 *March 2010*

78 1D mk III, 500 mm, f13, 1/1600s, ISO 1600 *March 2009*

80 1D mk III, 300 mm, f6.3, 1/1600s, ISO 1600
March 2009

82 1Ds mk II , 500 mm + 1.4x extender, f5.6, 1/80s, ISO 400
October 2005

83 1D mk IV, 300 mm, f6.3, 1/5000s, ISO 1250
February 2011

84 1D mk II, 500 mm, f4, 1/2500s, ISO 800
December 2005

85 1D mk II, 500 mm + 1.4x extender, f7.1, 1/400s, ISO 320
May 2006

86 & 87 1D mk II, 500 mm, f4, 1/1600s (86)/1/500s (87), ISO 640 *February 2006*

88 1D mk IV, 300 mm, f3.5, 1/3200s, ISO 1600
February 2010

90 1D mk IV, 500 mm, f4, 1/1250s, ISO 2500
January 2010

91 1D mk IV, 500 mm, f5.6, 1/500s, ISO 1250
January 2010

92 1D mk III, 800 mm, f5.6, 1/1000s, ISO1600
October 2008

93 1Ds mk II, 500 mm + 1.4x extender, f5.6, 1/400s, ISO 400
December 2004

94 1D, 500 mm, f4, 1/800s, ISO 400 *December 2003*

95 1D mk IV, 800 mm, f5.6, 1/400s, ISO 2000
October 2010

96 & 97 1D mk IV, 800 mm, f7.1, 1/4000s, ISO 1600 (96)/ISO 1250 (97)
February 2011

98 & 99 1D mk IV, 800 mm, f8 (98)/ f9 (99), 1/2000s, ISO 1000 *April 2010*

100 1D mk II, 500 mm, f5, 1/1250s, ISO 500 *June 2006, Iceland*

101 1D mk IV, 800 mm, f5.6, 1/1600s, ISO 1250
January 2011

102 1D mk II, 500 mm, f5, 1/2000s, ISO 500 *April 2006, Norway*

103 1D mk IV, 500 mm, f8, 1/1600s, ISO 800
November 2010, Spain

104 1D mk III, 500 mm, f8, 1/2500s, ISO 1250 *April 2009, Norway*

105 1D mk II, 300 mm f6.3, 1/2000s, ISO 320 *March 2005*

106 1D mk IV, 500 mm, f5, 1/3200s, ISO 1250
March 2010, Norway

108 1D mk III, 300 mm, f4.5, 1/3200s, ISO 1600 *May 2008, Hungary*

109 1D mk III, 800 mm, f9, 1/2500s, ISO 1000
February 2009

110 1D mk III, 500 mm, f8, 1/250s, ISO 500 *May 2008, Hungary*

111 1D mk III, 500 mm, f4.5, 1/2500s, ISO 2000 *June 2008*

112 1D mk II, 500 mm + 1.4x extender, f11, 1/2000s, ISO 200 *April 2006*

113 1D mk III, 500 mm, f8, 1/2500s, ISO 1250 *April 2009, Norway*

114 & 115 1D mk IV, 500 mm, f8 (114)/ f6.3 (115), 1/2000s (114)/1/4000s (115), ISO 800 *November 2010, Spain*

116 1D mk II, 500 mm, f4.5, 1/2000s, ISO 400 *July 2004, Norway*

117 1D mk II, 500 mm + 1.4x extender, f6.3, 1/3200s, ISO 500 *September 2006*

118 1D mk III, 70–200 mm (85 mm), f7.1, 1/2500s, ISO 1600 *February 2008*

119 1D mk II, 500 mm, f6.3, 1/2500s, ISO 400 *November 2004, United Arab Emirates*

120 1D mk III, 500 mm + 1.4x extender, f7.1, 1/2500s, ISO 1600 *April 2008*

121 1D mk IV, 70–200 mm (140 mm), f8, 1/3200s, ISO 1600 *March 2010*

122 1D mk II, 500 mm + 1.4x extender, f5.6, 1/3200s, ISO 400 *March 2006*

124 1Ds mk II, 500 mm, f4, 1/640s, ISO 800 *May 2007*

125 1D mk II, 500 mm, f4, 1/400s, ISO 800 *April 2006*

126 1D mk II, 300 mm, f2.8, 1/320s, ISO 1250 *May 2006*

128 1D mk III, 500 mm, f8, 1/1250s, ISO 800
September 2007

129 1D mk III, 800 mm, f5.6, 1/1600s, ISO 1600
October 2008

130 1D mk II, 500 mm + 1.4x extender, f7.1, 1/2000s, ISO 500 *March 2007, Norway*

132 1Ds mk III, 24 mm, f8, 1/800s, ISO 250 *April 2009, Norway*

133 1D mk III, 35 mm, f2, 1/50s, ISO 3200 *October 2008*

134 1D mk III, 300 mm, f3.2, 1/1250s, ISO 1600
January 2008

135 1D mk III, 300 mm, f2.8, 1/640s, ISO 1000
January 2008

136 1D mk II, 300 mm + 1.4x extender, f5.6, 1/1000s, ISO 200 *June 2004*

137 1D mk II, 500 mm, f32, 1/200s, ISO 320 *April 2005*

138 1D mk III, 500 mm + 2.0 extender, f8, 1/800s, ISO 1600 *July 2008, Norway*

139 1D mk IV, 800 mm + 1.4x extender, f11, 1/200s, ISO 800 *January 2010, Canada*

140 1D mk IV, 800 mm, f5.6, 1/160s, ISO 1600
January 2011

141 1D mk IV, 500 mm, f4.5, 1/500s, ISO 2000
January 2011

142 1Ds mk III, 70–200 mm (70 mm), f8, 1/2500s, ISO 800
March 2010, Norway

143 1Ds mk III, 800 mm + 1.4x extender, f10, 1/400s, ISO 500 *September 2009, Spain*

144 1D mk III, 800 mm, f18, 1/4000s, ISO 1600
March 2009, Spain

145 1D mk III, 70–200 mm (185 mm), f3.5, 1/640s, ISO 1600 *April 2009, Norway*

146 1D mk IV, 500 mm, f9, 1/1250s, ISO 1250
November 2010, Spain

147 1D mk IV, 800 mm + 1.4x extender, f29, 1/160s, ISO 800
February 2011

148 1D mk IV, 500 mm f6.3, 1/4000s, ISO 800
November 2010, Spain

150 1D mk IV, 800 mm + 1.4x extender, f8, 1/250s, ISO 400
May 2010

151 1Ds mk II, 500 mm + 2.0x extender, f16, 1/400s, ISO 400 *April 2007, Sweden*

152 1D mk III, 500 mm, f7.1, 1/2000s, ISO 1600 *April 2009, Norway*

154 1D mk III, 800 mm + 1.4x extender, f22, 1/125s, ISO 500 *March 2009*

156 1Ds mk III, 800 mm + 1.4x extender, f10, 1/400s, ISO 500 *February 2010*

157 1Ds mk III, 500 mm + 2.0x extender, f10, 1/640s, ISO 500 *May 2008, Hungary*

INDEX